A Geisha's Journey

A Geisha's Journey

MY LIFE AS A KYOTO APPRENTICE

PHOTOGRAPHS BY Naoyuki Ogino

TEXT BY Komomo

Translated by Gearoid Reidy and Philip Price

KODANSHA INTERNATIONAL
Tokyo • New York • London

Distributed in the United States by Kodansha America Inc., and in the United Kingdom and continental Europe by Kodansha Europe Ltd.

Published by Kodansha International Ltd., 17–14 Otowa 1-chome, Bunkyo-ku, Tokyo 112–8652, and Kodansha America Inc.

First edition, 2008
17 16 15 14 13 12 11 10 09 08   10 9 8 7 6 5 4 3 2 1

    Library of Congress Cataloging-in-Publication Data

Ogino, Naoyuki, 1975-
  A geisha's journey : my life as a Kyoto apprentice / photographs by Naoyuki Ogino ; text by Komomo ; translated by Philip Price and Gearoid Reidy. -- 1st ed.
    p. cm.
  ISBN 978-4-7700-3067-2
  1. Komomo--Pictorial works. 2. Geishas--Japan--Kyoto--Pictorial works.
3. Geishas--Japan--Kyoto--Biography--Pictorial works. I. Komomo. II. Title.
  GT3412.7.K65O45 2008
  792.702'80952--dc22
                    2007041043

www.kodansha-intl.co.jp

CONTENTS

The entrance of the Kaden Geiko House

FOREWORD

*I*n late fall of 1998, I received an e-mail from a young man named Ogino: "I would like to take some photographs of a *maiko*," it read. I was both amused and intrigued by his directness, and so I agreed to meet him.

He arrived a few days later, holding two photographs. As I had suspected, in person he was much more mild-mannered and polite than his initial correspondence suggested. The two photographs were of a cactus and a girl, and he explained that he had taken them both in the Mexico town where he lived. The moment I laid eyes on them I realized, for the first time, that a photograph can be a work of art. Not only had he captured the image of a beautiful Mexican girl, but he had also seen inside her heart; somehow, with just a single picture, he had told the story of her life. I was filled with curiosity about how this talented young man would tell the story of our world. That day turned out to be the first of many meetings with Ogino-*kun*, as he came affectionately to be known.

It was more than a year earlier, in the spring of 1997, that I had received my first e-mail from the young woman who would become the subject of this book. I had just set up my own website, the first of any working *geiko*, and an article had been written about me in a newspaper. Somehow, this article had found its way to faraway Beijing and the home of a certain little Japanese girl.

"I believe I was born to be a maiko," read the e-mail. Her elegant writing and rich expressiveness were those of a rather romantic girl, perhaps a fan of historical novels, just as I had been when I was a child. I sent a brief reply, thanking her for taking the time to look at my website, and almost immediately received another message in return: "How kind of you to take the time to write when you must be so busy. Receiving a reply from you is like a dream come true!"

Thus began a correspondence that lasted three years. I answered all her questions about life as a maiko, and she told me all about her upbringing and her daily life. Even through the lifeless computer fonts, her sentences painted a vivid picture of a highly sensitive, perceptive girl, and I came to look forward to her e-mails as if they were installments of a serialized novel.

Two years later, she came to Kyoto to try her hand at life in our *hanama-chi*, the Miyagawa-cho geiko district. Training as a maiko is unimaginably hard for the spoiled children of today's society, and in an attempt to reduce the number of dropouts, we have set up a system of work experience where girls who are interested in becoming maiko can stay with us for a week and get a taste for the life. All the girls are fascinated by the maiko at first, but many end up torn between training or going back to school. Komomo was different. From the very first moment, there was a special spark in her eyes, and I think this spark has been captured perfectly by the lens of Ogino-kun's camera.

The hanamachi were created as places of healing. The beautiful kimono and hair ornaments, the traditional dances to the sound of the shamisen, the gentle smiles of the geiko and maiko—all are aimed at lifting the hearts of our customers. This culture of healing has been developed and refined over hundreds of years, and it is the job of a maiko to embody its principles, or, in other words, to learn how to lift hearts simply by her presence. One thing that can't be learned, however, is an ability to feel. A person who can feel the joy of something beautiful and the pain of something sad is almost like a mind reader—she is capable of sharing happiness and hurt, she knows what to say and how to say it, and she can repair wounded hearts. The best maiko all have this ability.

In the spring following her first experience of hanamachi life, the girl with the spark in her eyes returned, carrying a small suitcase filled with her dreams of becoming the most *Japanese* girl in the whole of Japan.

Maiko training begins by learning how to say "hello." The trainee must greet the other person as an adult human being. She must be able to assess their position, and her own, and speak accordingly. Her demeanor—or as we say here in Kyoto, her *motenashi*—must be perfect at all times. From the moment she wakes up to the moment she lays her head on the pillow at the end of the day, there is no time for a maiko to slouch. From the depths of her heart to the tips of her hair, she must always act as someone who lives in the hanamachi. Once she has become accustomed to these concepts, the real training begins—dancing, singing, playing the shamisen, and more. This is a difficult time for all trainees, no matter how dedicated or talented, and they often become confused and disheartened.

Komomo was no exception, and one day during her early days of training as a lowly *shikomi*, she seemed to be on the verge of giving it all up. On that very day Kyoto was awash in cherry blossoms, and as we walked through the tunnels of pale pink flowers on the banks of the Kamo River and the Takase Canal, she cried out, "Oh, it's so beautiful! There are no cherry blossoms in Beijing." It was as if the spark in her eyes had been relit by the beautiful images reflected in them, as if each tiny flower had the power to touch the human heart. If indeed a flower has such a power, then surely it must come directly from their roots deep below the earth that struggle unseen to take in goodness from their surroundings day by day, unstintingly, never giving up. . . .

In the summer of 2000, a flower blossomed in my home when Komomo became a maiko, as pretty as a little sunflower standing proudly upright from mother earth. I will leave the telling of her story from that moment onward to Ogino-kun and his unusual lens, cold and clear on the surface, but filled with human warmth.

Ikuko Takeda (Koito)
Kaden Geiko House

PREFACE: Childhood Dreams

I am Japanese. I was born in Mexico, where my parents were living at the time. It had been their intention to settle down to life in a foreign country and try as hard as they could to fit in, but they also told me that they always kept in mind how important it was not to lose their identity as Japanese people. They used to joke that they were like eggs, white on the outside but yellow on the inside. After I was born, they realized that I wouldn't have a Japanese identity unless they made an effort to get me interested in the culture and the language. The funny thing is, they were so successful in immersing me in all things Japanese that I guess I became yellow inside and out.

I was still very young when we moved back to Japan. Sometimes my parents and my grandmother would dress me in kimono, which I loved. My parents also encouraged me to learn ballet, but what I really wanted to learn was *Nihon-buyo*, or traditional Japanese dance. As I grew more interested in Japanese culture, I persuaded my parents to let me visit Kyoto, Japan's ancient capital. I completely fell in love with the city and all its traditional culture.

As I grew older, my fascination became deeper and deeper, eventually leading me to the *hanamachi*, or geisha districts, and the *geiko*, as they call geisha in Kyoto. To me, they seemed the very definition of style and sophistication. I was desperate to find out more about these beautiful women, but they were almost never mentioned in books and magazine articles, and I began to realize how little information there was about the geiko and their way of life. Before long I came to a dead end. Since I came from a regular

My fascination with geisha began when I was very young. But I put those dreams aside, and went to Beijing with my family because it seemed like a way to expand my way of thinking and my values. And it did in many ways. I commuted to school by bicycle, which scared me at first. I must have been a huge nuisance to the other cyclists and drivers until I got used to the pace of the crowded roads.

II

My cat made the move to Beijing with my family. Her name was Momo, which means "peach." A few years later, when I became a *maiko* apprentice, I was given the name Komomo, which means "little peach," in a pure coincidence.

working family with no connection to the hanamachi, there was no way to learn more. The world of the geiko seemed to exist behind a veil, completely closed off from ordinary people like me.

When I was in sixth grade, after searching through piles of phone books, I finally found a teacher to teach me Nihon-buyo. It was like entering a different world, putting on my kimono and dancing every day.

But I studied for less than a year. Just when I had finished elementary school, my parents suddenly asked if I was interested in going to live in China. My father was being transferred, and so I put aside my thoughts about becoming a geiko and agreed at once.

One reason I decided to go was that I wanted to see how people in other countries lived. It seemed to me that the people around me in Japan didn't have their own thoughts or ideas. My classmates were like sheep, copying what everyone else did. They lined up to do whatever was popular, like taking "print club" pictures and buying the newest fad, but I never felt this desire to follow them blindly. I had often wondered if it was only Japanese people who were like this, and I figured that if I went somewhere like China, maybe I could put my theory to the test.

But at first, I couldn't communicate with anyone. Stupidly, I had gone to China without studying any Chinese. I only knew how to say "hello" and "thank you." I went to a regular Chinese school, but I couldn't keep up with my classmates, or even understand anything they said to me. It was the hardest time in my life, and every day I left school in tears.

My school had a special class for foreign students. There were a few other Japanese students, but the biggest group was the Koreans. Even though we looked the same, our ways of thinking were totally different. They knew a lot about politics and had a much stronger national identity than we Japanese did. One day one of the Korean students asked me if I knew Takeshima, the

Being in the midst of a very different culture played a part in my decision to become an apprentice *geiko*. I was in Beijing when I found the website of the "elder sister" whose geiko house I would eventually join to begin my journey.

island in the Sea of Japan that is claimed by both Japan and Korea. There were two or three other Japanese students there, but none of us really knew anything about the place or its history. When the Koreans said that Takeshima belonged to them, we couldn't think of anything to say back to them, so we just said, "Sure, go ahead. Take it."

When I thought about it later, though, I got kind of annoyed. Compared with the other students, we didn't really know much about our own country or culture, and so we ended up coming across as timid and weak. I suppose you could say that those experiences in China made me even more determined to become a geiko. I wanted to be a Japanese person who could explain her own country and culture to others.

At that time, I really felt like I wanted to wear a kimono all the time, not just on special occasions. I thought that was what Japanese people should do, so I brought nearly a dozen kimono with me to China, most of which I had gotten from my grandmother's storehouse in the country. Some of them had been hidden away for decades and had gotten old and worn, but I thought they were beautiful and wore them regularly.

In reality, though, it was pretty unusual for a girl my age to wear kimono all the time—lots of my friends had never even worn one once, let alone owned so many. One day, a television crew who wanted to film students from different countries wearing their national dress came to our school. Of course, the Koreans and the others all came wearing their national costume, but none of my Japanese friends had brought any kimono to China. Even the families who did bring them only had expensive kimono for special occasions, not the kind you would let a child wear. Thanks to my grandmother, though, I had enough for everybody.

The turning point in my life came when my mother showed me a newspaper article about a woman named Koito, the first Kyoto geiko to start her

The first six months in China were the hardest in my life. I hadn't studied Chinese before going, so I had a very difficult time catching up with my classmates. This photo was taken in my Chinese language class; I studied very hard, though I often cried from frustration.

own website. I immediately looked it up, and found everything I had been looking for—the real details about them, the things that weren't written in any of the books. I was so excited that I e-mailed Koito-san straight away, telling her that I wanted to become a *maiko*, an apprentice geiko, but that I didn't know where to begin. You can probably imagine how happy and surprised I was when she sent a reply telling me she would get me started.

Koito-san and I began to write regularly, but actually becoming a maiko still seemed like a distant dream. Then, in one of her e-mails, Koito-san wrote, "I can really see a spark of talent in you." This kind comment made me realize it was time to make up my mind, and I began to ask myself if I truly had what it would take to make my dream come true.

A little while later, I was talking to two of my Japanese school friends who knew about my desire to become a maiko. I told them what Koito-san had said, and about something else I had read—that the training is so tough that only one girl in three actually succeeds in becoming a maiko. One of them said, "Okay, so take the three of us. If we were the ones in maiko training, you'd be pretty confident about making it then, right?" Her words really made me believe in myself, made me realize that success or failure had nothing to do with mathematical probability, and everything to do with my own will to succeed. If this was truly what I wanted to do, I would see it through to the end.

I continued to e-mail Koito-san, and during the winter holidays in my last year of junior high school, we decided I'd go to Kyoto to her own, brand-

There weren't many places for kids to play in China, no arcades and few karaoke clubs. Playing pool and going to parks were the only things you could do for enjoyment. I used to play pool a lot on weekends. I never learned the official way to play, though; we had our own rules.

new *okiya*, or geiko house. It would be a sort of interview for the both of us, to get to know one another.

I was so nervous and excited to meet Koito-san that even though I had so many things I wanted to ask, I ended up asking totally dumb questions, like if she was tired when she got home from work. But far more important than the questions were the things I saw there. When I saw a maiko in person for the first time, I was overcome by her beauty. Just being in the okiya, in the middle of that world I had dreamed about for so long, was enough to settle it for me.

My mind was made up. Before another year went by, I left my parents in China and went to Kyoto to train under Koito-san. It was the beginning of my long-awaited adventure as a maiko on her way to becoming a geiko. I was fifteen years old.

The First Steps

The first time I saw my name on a plaque at the entrance to the *geiko* house (LEFT) was a very happy moment. My *oneesan* didn't say anything; she just put it up and left it there for me to see. The new wood looked so clean and beautiful, I felt like I'd really entered a different world.

The *misedashi* is the first time we have our makeup done by a professional (RIGHT). When I was still a beginner apprentice, I was always running around taking care of people. On the day of the misedashi, everyone was focused on me. I felt like a bride on her wedding day.

Once I'd set my heart on becoming a *maiko*, my parents tried to warn me about how tough the training would be and how lonely I would feel. In the end, though, they didn't really stand in my way. I was an only child, so I figured they would probably miss me a little, but I was determined to make it.

Koito-san's *okiya* is in Miyagawa-cho, one of the five famous *hanamachi* districts in Kyoto, and this is where I headed with my parents to meet and talk with her about what was ahead. Trainees are usually supposed to call the head of their geiko house *okaasan*, or "mother," but because Koito-san was still an active geiko, I called her *oneesan*; this literally means "elder sister," but both terms can be used to refer to the people responsible for teaching and mentoring apprentices. At the meeting, my dad asked what my "stage name" would be. Koito-san decided that she would take the *ko*, which means "small," from her own name and add it to *momo*, which means "peach." So I ended up as Komomo—"Little Peach." She chose peach because my face is round, and also because Japanese people associate peaches with China, where I had lived. Funnily enough, my cat's name was also Momo, and my school friends used to call me Momo-chan too. Since it was already my nick-

I don't remember exactly when this was taken, but this is me with my oneesan soon after I joined the geiko house, or *okiya*. It's during the summer, since I'm wearing a *yukata*, the simplest form of kimono. You can tell by my face that I'm still just a child.

name, I was really happy with Komomo—to be honest, I think it suits me much better than my real name, Ruriko. My dad seemed happy too.

Maiko training was pretty tough. It meant losing all the freedoms I'd taken for granted in my old life. I never knew when I could see my family, or even when I'd be allowed a day off. In the first stage we are called *shikomi*, which basically means "trainee." I wore regular clothes, not a kimono, and had to do lots of chores around the okiya and the hanamachi. As a newcomer, I had to introduce myself to all the people in the district who would help me in the years to come. Most important among these were the owners of the *ochaya*, the tea houses where the geiko attend engagements. It was all kind of a blur—I never knew who I was introducing myself to. But they all knew who I was, and I could tell they were watching my every move.

As a shikomi, I had to stay up late until Koito-san came home. She was a full geiko, which meant that most nights she attended evening parties called *ozashiki*. Ozashiki usually take place at one of the tea houses, although they are sometimes held in restaurants and hotels. Geiko are hired to entertain and perform for the guests, and we're also expected to pour drinks and enter into conversations. But all that was far away in my future. For the time being, I had to content myself with helping Koito-san into and out of her

For the first two weeks after I passed the exam to become a maiko, I was known as a *minarai*. This stage of training is very short—only two weeks—and it passed in a blur of training while I tried to absorb all that was going on around me. I don't really remember much about it.

kimono and joining her for meals when she returned, usually at about two in the morning.

The rest of my time was spent just getting used to everything. I soon realized that the main point of my existence as a shikomi was to help people. This was a big shock to me—my parents had never really made me do much housework, but suddenly it seemed my only role was to make life easier for others.

This meant changing the way I dealt with people. The first problem was my accent. I spoke standard Tokyo Japanese, and it was hard to change my intonation to the peculiar dialect spoken in the Kyoto hanamachi, which sounds very cute. I was told to bow and greet everyone I met on the street, which was very difficult for me, first of all because I was so shy, and secondly because everyone knew *me*, but I didn't know a thing about *them*.

Every day when I got up and went to sleep, I had to say, "Good morning oneesan" or "Good night oneesan" to Koito-san. If I had an upcoming appointment, I had to say "Tomorrow *otano moshimasu*," which is a humble phrase to ask the other person's favor. If I had been asked to help her do something at a party that day, I had to say, "Thank you for today, oneesan." If I forgot to say it, I would get scolded. This continued throughout my years as a maiko and became so ingrained that I still do it today.

Even though the training was tough, there was only one time when it got to the point where I wanted to quit. There was another girl who joined Koito-san's okiya about the same time as I did. As shikomi, we did all the same things and spent all our time together. She was quite a bit older than me,

If I look a little anxious (LEFT) it's because I'm rushing to take part in my first Japanese flute performance, and I was so nervous my lips were quivering! I don't remember making any big mistakes, but I definitely could have played better.

I was just as nervous when the *oshiroiya* was coating my face and neck with the white powder for my misedashi (RIGHT). I was wondering what I'd look like in full maiko makeup.

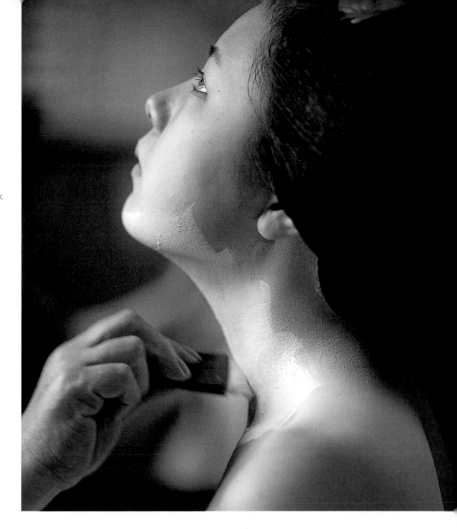

and since I had no sister of my own, I really looked up to her. But after only two weeks of training, she told Koito-san that she wanted to leave—and I said I wanted to go home too.

Koito-san just looked at me. She said, "Are you sure you're not just copying her?" That made me stop and think. I realized that I really didn't want to quit at all. I thought again about my original reasons for coming, and swore that no matter what happened, I would stay for at least six months. So from that time on it was just the two of us, Koito-san and me.

Nevertheless, I refused to feel sad, or lonely, or homesick. I had already experienced true loneliness in my first six months in China. That was the hardest time in my life—I felt so sad that I cried every day. Coming to Kyoto was my choice; I had come here to realize my dreams. And besides, there was so much to learn and so many new things to figure out that I didn't have enough time to wallow in self-pity. It's hard to change your own personality, but if that's what it took to succeed as a maiko, I was willing to give it a go.

After six months of studying, learning, and practicing, it was time to take the exam to become a maiko (since then the system has changed to ten months). It was the scariest thing I had ever done—I was so nervous my hands were shaking. For the exam I had to perform two dances, but perfect dancing wasn't nearly enough to pass. Everything from my manners to my way of walking was under scrutiny. Before the exam, I had to greet and serve tea to my examiners—various older geiko, some okiya owners, teachers, and members of the committee that administers the geiko district—one by one. As I served them, I asked them, "Otano moshimasu." I knew all their eyes were on me, watching the way I poured the tea and the way I sat down, and listening to every word I said.

I did the two dances, bowed, and thanked everyone. I felt sure I had passed, but Koito-san looked worried. She wasn't concerned with whether I had passed the test or not; what troubled her was my future as a maiko—my manners, my poise, and my behavior in the world of the hanamachi. I told her afterward how nervous I had been during the exam, but she just replied, "What are you talking about? It's from now that things get tough."

Sure enough, I passed the test, which enabled me to become a *minarai*, or apprentice. Now I could accompany my oneesan to her appointments to learn about her work. This stage of training is very short, only two weeks, and to be honest I can't remember much about it. One thing that has stayed with me, though, is the first time I was allowed to dress in a full kimono. At the same time I had my hair done up in the traditional Japanese style,

(ABOVE) I must be checking to see if the scratch on my cheek by the house's cat was visible. I'm sure he thought he was supporting me on my big day, but I ended up looking like a scarred gangster.

This day was also the first time I got to wear the traditional black-crested kimono with long sleeves (RIGHT). You try not to be nervous with everyone's eyes on your every move!

which takes over an hour. I thought it looked beautiful, but it felt so large I was scared that the sides would catch on the telephone poles as I walked along the street. I also had to practice putting on *oshiroi*, the maiko's white makeup. These days, of course, most junior high school girls are used to wearing makeup, but for me it was a completely new experience. This also takes about an hour to apply, and when I looked in the mirror, it was like staring at a different person.

During this period I started accompanying Koito-san to her evening banquets. We would travel by taxi from one *ochaya* to the next and make appearances at lots of ozashiki in front of people I had never met. The time passed by in a whirl, and soon a more important ceremony loomed ahead: my *misedashi*, the ceremony to mark my debut as a maiko. As a maiko, I would start working—and studying—on my own.

I spent the whole day before the ceremony preparing with my oneesan. There were so many tiny little details to take care of. Koito-san prepared my clothes for the ceremony and ironed out all the wrinkles. I had to make the rounds of all the tea houses in the area, asking for their support, and every night, before I slept, I had to make sure to ask Koito-san for her support. "Otano moshimasu."

The day of the ceremony was crazy; I didn't have a moment to myself. There was a way of doing everything, and since it was all new to me I could only follow directions from others; I couldn't do anything myself. I wore a very formal black kimono and spent the whole day stressed out about silly little things: from the scratch on my face that my oneesan's cat had been kind enough to inflict on me the night before, to making sure I didn't spill anything on my kimono.

Older geiko and a committee member came to watch my oneesan and me exchange cups of sake. I was very tense, conscious of my every move, but I got through it by watching my oneesan closely and copying her movements. After the ceremony, when I first stepped outside as a maiko, there was a huge crowd of people standing there waiting to see me, holding cameras and taking pictures.

I felt like a movie star. I had to go around all the different tea houses once more, and then had one ozashiki after another, including one with my parents and another just for a photo shoot. I spent only fifteen or twenty minutes at each, not performing but just staying long enough for the customers to drink a glass of beer. I remember a television crew taking footage of me and asking me how I felt. All I could think of to say was that it was really hard work.

I wore the black formal kimono for three days and a different formal kimono for three days after that. On the seventh day after my misedashi, I dressed in a standard maiko's kimono. My life was now the life of a maiko.

During my *misedashi*, I had to visit all of the hanamachi geiko houses and greet the owners. There are about forty okiya in Miyagawa-cho, so you can imagine how tiring it was to visit them in the middle of summer, wearing my heavy kimono and in full makeup. It took quite a while to make the rounds, so the conversations with the owners were pretty short. I'd just poke my head in the door, introduce myself, and ask for their support in the future. They all knew I was coming, so they just briefly congratulated me and wished me luck. Then I was off to the next one. Lots of people came up to me on the street to congratulate me.

During the misedashi ceremony, one of the Miyagawa-cho geiko house owners (RIGHT) acted as a kind of go-between for an exchange of sake cups. My oneesan and I sat opposite each other, and the go-between passed the cups between us. Once the trainee has exchanged cups of "sake" (actually non-alcoholic since it's just symbolic), she has become a full member of the hanamachi.

The lady accompanying me is an *obachan* from one of the Miyagawa-cho "offices." The obachan takes care of new maiko, accompanying them on their tour of the tea houses during the misedashi, and looking after them over their careers.

A Hanamachi Education

All the songs we learn are written in books like this one (LEFT); they don't look anything like Western music notation. First, our teacher sings the song for us, and as we listen and learn, we write the words of the song, drawing special symbols for when to go high, low, or so on.

During the New Year period (RIGHT) we perform a special dance to ask the gods for a good rice harvest and fertility in the coming year. We ring these special bells shaped like branches bearing fruit and wear hair ornaments made of rice stalks to show our respect for Japan's staple food.

The rules of the *hanamachi* world were completely different than those of the world I had come from. There was so much I had to learn as a *maiko*, and so many duties to perform. Every day I was faced with things I didn't understand; sometimes it seemed as if the streets of Miyagawa-cho were peppered with land mines just waiting to explode in my face. It was like being at school twenty-four hours a day, seven days a week.

A maiko's schedule is very fixed. In the evening, I would attend *ozashiki* from around six until late, and every morning I would wake up around ten. After dressing in my less formal kimono, I had practice in the performing arts, and at lunchtime, I paid visits to each of the almost forty tea houses in Miyagawa-cho, where many of the ozashiki were held. Believe it or not, I did this every day for two whole years, just to drum up business for our *okiya*.

The hanamachi has its own peculiar traditions—one of which is that you don't knock on the tea house door before entering. Instead, I would just open the front door and let myself into the entrance hall. If I saw the *okaasan* of the tea house in the back, I would go inside and say, "Hello, mother. *Otano moshimasu.*" And of course, "Thank you."

Even the rules for day-to-day greetings are fixed. No matter how young the owner of the tea house was, I had to call her "mother," and no matter how old a *geiko* was, I was supposed to greet her as "older sister." At first I could never tell whether the person I had just met on the street was a tea house owner or a geiko, and I often ended up calling geiko "mother" and tea house owners "sister."

On my visits, the okaasan and I would chat about the weather and little things like that. I would thank her for a previous party I had attended at her tea house or request her help if we had one coming up, and then I would leave. If there was no one in the tea house, I would leave a letter saying the same kinds of things, and before leaving I would tidy up the owner's shoes in the entrance hall. I learned to go through all the houses in order, so that I never left one out.

Some of the rooms where *ozashiki* are held are very small; we end up having to dance and play the shamisen in a space the size of a single tatami mat, with the customers' faces literally inches away from us. At those times, it's important to be able to think fast and be flexible, but even then it's sometimes impossible to avoid touching the customers with our kimono.

The biggest part of my life at that time was taken up with practice. As a maiko, I was expected to learn to sing and play the shamisen, play rhythmical instruments, perform the tea ceremony, and, of course, dance. Dance practice was the one I had to concentrate on most. A maiko has to learn two different dances for every month of the year to perform for the customers at ozashiki. Practicing a dance until we knew it by heart was vital—the first time I had to dance at an ozashiki, I was so nervous that my mind went totally blank!

Even though practice is tough, I love to dance. I think dance is universal. Everyone has a desire to move in time to the sound of voices and instruments. Unlike ballet, which is based on jumping and flying into the air, Nihon-buyo comes from our roots as agricultural people and from our worship of the gods of the earth. It is based on bringing our feet down and connecting with the ground. When the movements of the dance combine with the music and lyrics, customers can easily understand whether we're crying, or enjoying ourselves, or feeling sad. To me, that's what dance is all about.

Dance lessons take place at the *kaburenjo*, run by the Miyagawa-cho Ochaya Association. While I was a *shikomi*, the okiya paid for my practice sessions and decided what days and times I should practice. But once I'd become a maiko I could decide to take extra lessons, and I would have to

Yachiho-san, a *geiko* at Koito-san's *okiya*, Kosen-san, then a *maiko*, and I are learning a new song. A lot of the pieces we play are very old, but sometimes we are given a new piece to learn. They aren't usually written by just one person: a lyrics master writes the lyrics, the music master writes the melody, and then the dance master creates a dance to go with it. It can take up to a year to complete.

pay for them. As I mentioned before, I studied Nihon-buyo a little when I was young, and fortunately I'd managed to avoid picking up any bad habits.

We learn to dance by watching the master and trying to copy her moves. First we try to remember the basic steps; then, after the master has corrected our mistakes, we work on the details. We start in a group, and afterward we practice individually to correct our mistakes. Sometimes there would be ten or twenty maiko practicing together.

Learning just one dance took a long time. Each practice session was forty-five minutes to an hour long, and I had to do three or four sessions to figure out the basic steps of a single dance. At first, important dances like "The Ballad of Gion" or "Four Seasons in Kyoto" took me more than ten sessions to master. Nowadays I can learn a new dance in two practice sessions—just one for a short dance.

This is the manuscript for the new long song. It's based on the fifty-three stations of the Tokaido, the rest areas on the ancient Tokaido road from Tokyo to Kyoto. We perform both long epic songs and short songs: the long songs are kind of like mini-operas, containing lots of different melodies.

Needless to say, there were lots of rules to be followed at dance practice. As the youngest student, it was my responsibility to look after the dance master. That meant I had to pour her a new cup of tea when her cup was empty, and make sure she wasn't too hot or too cold. I also had to wait until all of the older students, whom we call *sempai*, had greeted her before I said hello.

When I started out as a maiko, I was terrified of my sempai; they were always getting mad at me for one reason or another, and it seemed as if I couldn't do anything right around them. Because I was so scared, I sometimes used to greet them before the master, or even before the customers at ozashiki. When this happened, of course, the sempai would get angry at me for not greeting the master or the customers first, making me even more fearful of them.

Looking back on it now, I would say that about ninety percent of my maiko education involved just trying to get through one difficult day after another. I didn't have any sense of the manners of the hanamachi, and I was constantly making mistakes. And the toughest part of all was treating my sempai correctly.

At one of my first ozashiki, for example, my sempai asked me in front of the customers what dance I would like to perform. When I answered cheerfully with the name of a dance I particularly liked, she suddenly got mad. Of course, now I know that her anger was part of my hanamachi education: in order to appear humble and modest, I should have declined to answer, asked her to decide for me, and then let her act as if the decision had been forced on her. In this way, neither of us would have appeared too pushy. I guess I just didn't have a clue back then.

Japanese society has lost touch with much of its traditional culture, and since I was a product of that society, lots of things about the hanamachi were completely alien to me. For example, I never heard the tones of a shamisen or the lyrics of traditional ballads when I was growing up. Old ballads, songs,

Each okiya hires an *otokoshi* to help us put on our kimono (RIGHT). There's never any flirtation between a geiko or a maiko and her dresser. Once she has started getting ready for an evening of ozashiki, she's already in work mode and romance is the last thing on her mind.

Maiko wear the wooden sandals (LEFT), called *okobo*. The color of the straps changes according to the status of the maiko. More-experienced maiko wear okobo with pink straps.

and poems are never on the radio or TV, so we never have a chance to hear them. At first, their rhythms and patterns and the special note that always comes at the end of a song sounded very weird. I had no natural sense for those things, so learning them was a real chore.

Then there's the language. It's easy enough to learn the ballads and poems by heart, but understanding their meaning is another matter. Classical Japanese has lots of words for describing emotions and senses that are part of the traditional Japanese spirit, so maybe if we were exposed to more of these songs and poems in modern Japan, there would be less of a gap between the modern and traditional societies. And then maybe it would be easier for girls to enter traditional worlds like that of the geiko.

Another thing that the masters complain about is that some of the movements of Nihon-buyo represent things that don't exist anymore, and so

are hard for young dancers to understand. Amazingly, there are some kids today who can't even understand the mime for sweeping with a broom!

I also wish more customers knew the meaning of the dances we perform, the symbolism of the changing patterns on our kimono, and the significance of the flowers we display. Sometimes we entertain customers who know all about these things, and at those times an ozashiki can be a wonderful occasion. The ones who understand the traditions and the arts can play with the lyrics of a song, for example, altering the lines to make them funny, or make up their own dances in time with the song. The number of people who can do that is shrinking, though, so most of the time we just end up playing simple party games that anyone can do.

Sometimes experienced customers give me advice or share some tricks of the trade. I remember one customer in particular. He was an eccentric old man from the countryside who sometimes said the strangest things, but one day he taught me an old kimono trick that I still use—how to stop my under-kimono from being seen when I'm dancing, which is considered rather rude.

It makes me a little sad that there are so few customers who know about the past, but I still have great hope that we Japanese can reconnect.

From January 5 until the *shigyoshiki* on January 7, we wear a special kimono. This period is always very busy for the *hanamachi*: there are lots of New Year's parties and then we have to get ready for the ceremony. (I love it when it snows in the hanamachi—it's cold, especially on the back of my neck where my kimono is open, but it looks so beautiful.)

Each hanamachi has its own symbol, or crest. Miyagawa-cho's crest is three interlinking circles, and this pattern is often printed onto lanterns hanging outside the tea houses and restaurants in the district (BELOW).

At the shigyoshiki ceremony (RIGHT), the most successful maiko and geiko of the previous year are given awards. Around December 25, each okiya receives a list of the people who are to be rewarded. In my second year, I only glanced at the list, never imagining I would be on it, so I was happy when I saw my name: once for being one of the ten most successful maiko and once for working so hard in my

dance and music lessons. My *oneesan* was really pleased that I'd received the award for my progress in the arts, but she wasn't so interested in the other award. "Most successful" basically means "made the most money," and my oneesan believes success has more to do with skill and less to do with earnings.

BOTTOM RIGHT: Remember the rice stalks that you can see in our hair ornaments? After the New Year's celebrations are over, we pass the seeds—three each—to our favored customers. It's said that if they keep them in their wallets, they'll be blessed with lots of money, so they're always eager to get them. If the seeds work and the customer has a good year, then of course he comes to ozashiki more often, so it works out well for everyone.

PAGES 42–43: At the shigyoshiki, we always sit in a particular order: maiko at the front, younger geiko in the middle, older geiko in back. I love seeing everyone sitting together—it looks fantastic!

We always bow to our audience at the beginning and end of every dance (LEFT). The form of the bow is very important—we have to cross our hands in front of our knees so that the fingers of each hand are lined up, and we have to make sure that we don't lift our bottom up off the floor. (In this photo, I'm just getting into position to start the bow, which is why I'm not yet sitting on the floor.) Maiko have the hardest time because the obi is so wide. It takes a lot of practice to get it right.

My oneesan always tells me that our job is to take
care of the hearts of our customers. In a way, we're
kind of like the doctors and nurses of the ozashiki:
we have to look after all of the guests and make sure
they have a wonderful experience and go away
feeling better. I love making people happy. Seeing
the smiles on their faces when we walk into the room
makes all the hard things about the life worthwhile.

The above photo was taken at a local restaurant. In the last couple of years, several nice restaurants have opened in Miyagawa-cho. They're casual, so we can just drop in for lunch or a snack after an afternoon engagement and relax. As soon as I drink anything hot, though, my lipstick gets smudged or comes off, so I always have to redo my makeup before I leave.

When my oneesan became a shamisen master, she gave a special performance at a restaurant. We have the same teacher, so a few of us were allowed to watch. It was great to be a member of the audience for once, rather than one of the performers.

PAGES 50–51: There are lots of performances throughout the year in addition to the big festivals and our regular ozashiki. Here, Kosen-san—another maiko from our okiya and my best friend—and I perform while Koito-san and our shamisen teacher flank us. These performances are held for people from the tea houses, other geiko, and any friends and family who are interested in the shamisen. We all learn the same songs, so we become very familiar with them, and that makes it fun to hear others perform them as well. Of course, we have to learn new songs for each performance, but I suppose if we had nothing to learn, we'd never practice.

Here (ABOVE), we're waiting in the wings before another performance. My nervousness lessened each time I performed.

Inside the House

The *otokoshi* always helps a *maiko* put on the most elaborate, formal kimono. But the also formal, but much simpler type of kimono I'm wearing (LEFT) I can do pretty much myself, though I have to use a mirror to make sure the collar is lined up correctly at the back of my neck. This style of kimono is called *karage*, and it's not difficult to put on.

I'm greeting a customer at the counter of our *okiya* (RIGHT). The tradition is to sit down on our heels outside the door, then open it and bow in greeting.

54

*L*ife in the *hanamachi* is all about relationships. With just the two of us in the *okiya*, we had to take extra care in maintaining good relationships with the owners of the surrounding tea houses, the masters who taught at the *kaburenjo*, the maids who worked in the tea houses, the kimono makers, and so many others. I guess we must have been successful, because the house was always bustling with people coming in and out—salesmen, older *geiko*, and, of course, our maids.

These days, not many regular Japanese families have maids, but our house was not a regular home—it was also a place of business. In the hanamachi, everyone was always pressed for time, and there wasn't a tea house around that didn't employ some help. Three people worked in our okiya, and they were like members of our family: the first was a woman who came every day to make our meals, arrange flowers, give us advice—she was also kind enough to mend our kimono, for example, when they got frayed. Another woman came to clean the house twice a week. Then, from seven to midnight every night, a third woman came and acted as kind of a backup for Koito-san and me, helping us at our counter, serving snacks, and making drinks for customers.

There was one other person whom we couldn't do without: the *otokoshi* dresser who helps us with our kimono. The dresser is usually male, and although you might be surprised to find that someone of the opposite sex is involved in such an intimate act, when you figure that a kimono can be up to twenty-three feet in length and weigh more than twenty-two pounds, you will probably realize that the dresser needs to be a man—and not just any man, but one strong enough to wrap the kimono so tight that it doesn't come loose even if we wear it for ten hours or more. He has to be gentle too, though, so that he doesn't hurt the woman he is dressing. And yes, the otokoshi helps us right from the underwear stage, although I can assure any man thinking about becoming a dresser that there is nothing even slightly erotic about the job! We are women on a mission; for us getting ready to go to work is like getting ready to go into battle. Every second counts.

On this day, I'd been out shopping with my friend Kohina-san. We were booked for the same *ozashiki* that evening, so she went back to her place and changed, and then she came over while I was changing into my kimono. It's kind of against the rules for maiko to go to one onother's places, but Kohina-san was also trained by Koito-san, so she's expected to check in with her every day. I suppose you could say it's her second home.

I must admit, though, at first it did feel a little strange being dressed by a man. But I soon realized that the dresser didn't look at me as just someone of the opposite sex, and in time I came to feel the same way about him. Eventually he became like a brother, someone to look out for me, someone I could ask for advice. Before the war, the dressers used to play a big role in a maiko's life. In those days, *maiko* were often very young, sometimes only ten years old, and if they fell asleep at an *ozashiki*, for example, it was the dresser who would carry them home. Even now in Gion's geiko district, the dresser accompanies a maiko on her visits to the tea houses when she starts out.

Over the years, more girls joined our okiya for maiko training. Kosen-san entered this world half a year after me, so she calls me "oneesan" even though we're the same age. The same with Yachiho-san, even though she's older than me (though I respect her as my *sempai* of life). You might think

Here I'm putting on *beni*, or lipstick, before going out to an ozashiki. At first, I would have to reapply it often, since it would come off when I ate or drank, but my *sempai* taught me how to put it on with two coats so it doesn't come off easily. Now I can make it through the day with just one application.

that women living together in a house would fight or have many troubles, but the relationship of rank is well established. Since *kohai* must follow the sempai's opinion whether they like it or not, it causes the sempai to take responsibility for their words. There are exceptions, of course, but in general the system works in keeping order.

I was an only child, so living together with other girls, sharing the good and the bad, made us more than real sisters. I've heard that even women who resign from the *hanamachi* world still keep a close relationship with their "sisters."

Life at the house got even busier. People would call to book us for lots of different engagements, and all of these were written down in our individual appointment books. I had to get into the habit of checking the book twice a day to make sure there hadn't been any last-minute changes.

In April we wear this special *kanzashi* hair ornament for the Kyo Odori, Miyagawa-cho's biggest dance performance of the year. This is the only time we paint our hands white (as well as our face), and it was also the only time as a maiko that Koito-san allowed me to use mascara. In my first year as a maiko, I was pretty bad at putting on makeup; you can see how hard I'm concentrating! At that time I had a room to myself, but in later years there were up to five girls in the same room, so it got pretty noisy—and messy—at times.

Even so, I never knew what the appointment involved until I arrived at the event itself. It could be a performance in front of a hundred people, or a one-on-one meeting with a customer. I might perform by myself or with half a dozen other geiko. It probably sounds like we're all really disorganized, but geiko don't really need to know anything other than the location. This is what we do every day, and it's not as if we would lower the quality of our work depending on the customers. At a really big party, the geiko might have a quick discussion to decide what dances we would perform, but even then we only need to get the basics in order. The details are left up to the *okaasan* of the tea house, who acts as a kind of agent between us and the customers.

Having put on my makeup and been dressed, I would head out for the evening. The first ozashiki usually began at about six, but first I went to the tea house that had arranged it to find out from the okaasan what time I would be picked up. The ozashiki were held in traditional restaurants, hotels, or in the tea house itself, but I usually had no idea where I was going until I got there.

Like everything else in hanamachi life, there are tons of rules to obey at an ozashiki. The newest and youngest maiko, who is around fifteen or sixteen years old, sits in the seat of honor; she is the center of attention at the start of the ozashiki.

It is her job to pay attention to things like changing the customers' ashtrays and making sure the beer keeps flowing. She has to make sure that glasses don't go empty and ashtrays don't get full.

Usually we start out with small talk about the weather or whether it's the first time for the customers to come to an ozashiki. Then we might talk about where they are from, although names and occupations tend to be no-go areas, especially if the customer is a local.

Of course, we don't spend all our time talking to the same customer. About halfway through the meal, we perform our dance, and after that everybody switches seats. We usually play it by ear—if a customer seems to have taken a liking to a particular girl, we leave them be. As the customers get more and more involved, we gradually move around the seats talking to

We tie the obi with a narrow strip of material called an *obijime*, and then tuck a special sash, known as an *obiage*, into the top of the obi. Even if I can't remember when a picture was taken, I always know what time of year it is from the kimono. Here the obiage is made of *ro*, a loosely woven silk fabric, so it must be summer. Thanks to global warming, it's getting harder to know when to bring out the winter kimono and put away the summer ones. Our okiya had a lot of different obijime and obiage for each season, and we were allowed to choose.

This is on one of the visits to the tea houses during the New Year's period. Of course, after Koito-san retired, she didn't come along anymore; it was just me, Kosen-san, and Yachiho-san. It felt really lonely at first without my oneesan. I remember following her to all the tea houses with a disposable camera on the day she told everyone about her retirement, taking lots of photos. Even though she'd made up her mind to retire, I think she was feeling a little sad, too.

different customers, until the most senior geiko is usually finally seated in the seat of honor.

When the ozashiki ended, at about eight, I would go back to the tea house that arranged it and thank the okaasan, and then, more often than not, I would go straight on to the tea house that was arranging the next one that night. On the rare occasions that I had nothing else penned in, I would go to a call-office and wait to be called out to another appointment. I would usually wait there until about midnight, and if nothing came up I would return to the okiya.

Having been busy practicing and working non-stop from ten that morning, my day was over at last, and I could take off the heavy kimono and thick white makeup I had been wearing since the afternoon. I did this myself, unless there was a *shikomi* in training at the time to help me. Then I could slide into a hot bath and finally get some sleep.

For the five years I was a maiko, this was my daily routine.

I can tell just from my feet and the bottom my kimono what time of day it is, what time of year it is (within three days), and where I'm going. This was taken between January 8 and January 10, and I'm heading out to an ozashiki. The underskirt of my kimono, which is called *juban*, is patterned in the *shibori* style, which we only wear after the *shigyoshiki* ceremony. It's my favorite style.

In my early years as a maiko, I was allowed to wear colorful kimono and hair ornaments like these, but as the years go by we are expected to gradually switch to more simple, sedately colored ones. It's a little difficult to see in the photo, but I have a peach *netsuke* hanging out of my obi. A netsuke is a little figure attached to a strap. A customer of mine found it in Heian Jingu, a famous shrine in Kyoto, and gave it to me as a present. Our netsuke is one of the few items of clothing we maiko are allowed to choose ourselves, and since this one matches my name, Komomo, it's very special to me.

Here we're crossing the Shijo Ohashi, which is a famous Kyoto bridge crossing the Kamo River. We were all trained by Koito-san and all have names starting with "Ko." I think this is a great picture—three maiko crossing the Shijo Ohashi with the Minamiza Theater behind us. It really sums up Kyoto.

This is a day that Kosen-san decided she wanted a *senjafuda*, which is a kind of good-luck charm, so we went out together to buy one. After we left this shop, we visited a craftsman to see some handmade goods. I'm too busy to go out very often, but when we do go shopping together we always have fun.

A few scenes from around the house: on this page
Kosen-san and I are playing one of the games that
we play with customers at ozashiki. Some of them
are just simple drinking games that anyone can play,
but when we get customers who know a lot about
hanamachi traditions, we often end up playing really
complicated word games using famous Japanese
songs.

PAGES 68–69: Whenever a new girl arrives at the
okiya, a new dressing table is set up for her. As you
can see, things get a little cramped. The dressing
table is our only personal space; everything else
is shared. At New Year's we replace the hanging
decoration over the dressing table for a new one.
The green kimono I'm wearing in this picture tells me
it was taken in December. At the end of that month,
we receive *fukudama*, which are balls filled with
small presents, each with its own special meaning.

Our house has a cat (ABOVE) who is very friendly, and we always play with him before the ozashiki start. He doesn't look too pleased here, though. A lot of the okiya keep dogs and cats. Since we live there together we become like a family, and I guess the pets become kind of like substitute children—it sometimes seems as if they are more important than the maiko and geiko! The cat at the right loved kimono. He used to get very jealous when we tried on new ones, and when we laid a kimono on top of him, he used to look in the mirror, all pleased with himself.

PAGES 72–73: This is a local restaurant in the hanamachi. It's very old and therefore protected by law. There are lots of different styles of houses in the hanamachi, and some of the carpentry techniques used in building them have been lost in the transition to modern Japan. The arch at the doorway to this restaurant is quite unusual, so I'm happy to know that it's protected.

PAGES 74–75: Yachiho-san, a geiko, is fixing my kanzashi. You can see here the big difference between the maiko and geiko hairstyles. The window behind us is covered by traditional Japanese blinds of wood and paper, known as *shoji*. The light coming through the Japanese paper is beautiful.

The Art of Performance

Throughout the year, we study dance according to the Wakayagi School, but for the Kyo Odori in April, we perform one dance—the finale—from another school called Umemoto. The way we move our fans and our bodies is different, so it always feels a little strange. It was nerve-wracking at first, but now I can switch between the styles without thinking.

The red color of the kimono I'm wearing (RIGHT) is considered a child's color, so only young *maiko* are supposed to wear it. But I loved it so much my *oneesan* let me wear it a little longer than I should have.

The daily routine of a *maiko*—and a *geiko*—stays fixed all year round; it's very rare for us even to be allowed to take public holidays off. Several times a year, though, our daily grind is broken by the excitement of the Kyoto festivals. Not only are these festivals important for bringing together the whole *hanamachi*, they are also great fun for us. The most important festival for us is the Kyo Odori, which is held in April. Another popular one is the flower parasol parade, or *hanagasa junko*, which is part of the famous Gion Festival in July. Ten local maiko are chosen each year from the area to take part in this parade.

Although I take part in the Kyo Odori every year, I was once lucky enough to be chosen for the Gion Festival. It was such a great honor and a really exciting opportunity for me, but to be honest, my biggest memories of it are how hot it was and how early we had to start in the morning. Despite the heat and the early start, though, it was fantastic to look out from the outdoor stage we were dancing on to see all the people, knowing that all their attention was on us.

The Kyo Odori is one of the few times that regular people get to see the geiko and maiko who live in the hanamachi. The roles for the festival are decided in January, and we start practicing the dances at the end of that month. By March, we are in dress rehearsal almost every day. Our hanamachi actually sponsors the event, so it would be seriously embarrassing if we messed it up. The first few times I was very nervous, but the other geiko and maiko always gave me lots of advice, so I tried my hardest not to disappoint them. It was also nice to spend time together with everyone backstage during the weeks of rehearsals—I made some really close friends that way.

The Kyo Odori gives me the opportunity to show everyone, including my parents, the progress I've made in my dancing throughout the year, but again it's the other stuff that stays in my mind, like how crazily busy we are all day. We must be at the hall in the morning, and yet we have to stay fully dressed in our makeup and kimono right until the end of our last *ozashiki* at night. The festival can be completely exhausting, both mentally and physically.

At my first Kyo Odori, I tucked a handkerchief into the sleeve of my kimono and must have forgotten about it. While we were on stage dancing, the handkerchief fell out of my pocket onto the stage. I thought it was no big deal and continued dancing. But backstage, after the performance, my oneesan came flying up to me looking furious. Only then did I realize what a big mistake I'd made. I had to apologize to everyone. It's not one of my happiest memories, to say the least.

In my first year, all I had to do was just say yes to everything I was told and try to stay out of trouble. But I climbed up the ranks each year until finally I was allowed to dance with just one other maiko, rather than as a part of the big group. Of course, my responsibilities increased at the same time. During practice, we are divided into groups with one maiko as a leader, and that maiko has to take responsibility for those under her, pointing out their mistakes, and making sure that they arrive on time and their manners are correct.

Every year my responsibilities as a maiko increased, and gradually I moved closer and closer to the day when I would have to make a huge decision.

This is the *ranma* at the Miyawaga-cho Theater (ABOVE), a decorative board made a century ago that is a transom between the ceiling and the stage. We're really lucky here in Miyagawa-cho to have one so beautiful and unique.

Part of the Gion Festival, the *hanagasa junko* (RIGHT) is a huge procession through the streets of Gion, another famous *hanamachi* in Kyoto. I was very lucky that year to be one of the few chosen to take part; I was even luckier to be able to sit in the front of the float.

At my first Kyo Odori in 2000, I danced the Miyagawa Ondo. The stage was really small and there were lots of other *geiko* and maiko dancing in front of me, behind me, and on both sides. I was constantly worried that I would crash into one of them and drop my fan.

PAGES 84–85: This is another photo of the performance of the Miyagawa Ondo. As you can see, the obi that the maiko wear are very long and bulky, so we're always worried that we're going to bump into each other. To avoid this, each of us has very fixed movements that we have to follow all the way through the performance.

The final three dances on the last day of the Kyo Odori are called the *senshuraku* (LEFT). For the very last dance, the older geiko join the performers on stage and paper cherry-blossom petals float down from the ceiling. I always love that moment. When the curtain falls, it brings with it a sense of relief that it's all over—at least for another year. After two months of practice, and two weeks of performances, I'm always exhausted—happy but exhausted.

The stage design represents Kiyomizu Temple, a famous Kyoto structure (ABOVE). Although the dances take place in spring and feature falling cherry blossoms, and the photo of the temple was taken in autumn, I still like the way it represents the link between nature and art.

Lots of people line the streets to watch
the hanagasa junko and some call out
compliments or shout out encouragement
for us to keep going. It's a lot of fun.

We do a pose (UPPER RIGHT) at the
start and end of every dance to let the
audience know that the dance is about
to start or has ended. We don't usually
bother doing this at a normal ozashiki
where there is no curtain or stage,
but at big performances this pose is a
fundamental part of the dance. I look
really nervous, probably beause of the
big crowd I'm about to perform for!

More New Year's photos. We're wearing our coats over our kimono (BOTTOM LEFT), probably because rain has been forecast. It's considered rude to wear them inside, so every time we go into a tea house, we have to take them off and drape them over our arm before we greet the *okaasan*. The older lady in the picture is a retired geiko who now runs a bar in the hanamachi.

As part of our New Years preparations, I gave one of these *kagami mochi* rice cakes (ABOVE), along with this piece of paper with my name on it, to my teachers, my tea house, and the go-between who helped with my *minarai*.

I can tell this was taken during the days leading up to the Kyo Odori, because of the lanterns that are hung up on the streets during this period. I'm heading off to an early ozashiki—they're usually held in the evening, but it's still light in this photo.

Decision Time

Once a *maiko* enters the last few weeks of her career as a maiko, her hair, makeup and clothes change completely. The *sakko* hairstyle is all set toward the back of the head (RIGHT), and it's hard to fix. Our entire maiko period we've been sleeping on a hard pillow with our hair hanging over the back. We've learned not to toss and turn too much during the night—to keep these hairstyles in one piece. The three lines at the back of our neck are called *sanbonashi*, which literally means "three legs."

I blackened my teeth (LEFT) for much of the period, and all the customers at the *ozashiki* wanted to see what they looked like.

When I first became a *maiko*, Koito-san and I agreed that I would live and work at the *okiya* for six years. Over those years, I had given a lot of thought to what I wanted to do when my period of service was over. I already had a lot of things I wanted to do: study abroad, learn English, and perhaps research Japanese culture and folklore. Strange though it may seem, becoming a full *geiko* had never crossed my mind, and I had never really spoken to Koito-san in detail about my future plans.

Around the start of my last year as a maiko, I finally plucked up the courage to tell Koito-san I was planning to quit the okiya without becoming a geiko. As we talked, I explained to her my dream of studying traditional culture and folklore. She never made the slightest objection to my decision. But she did say that if I truly wanted to let the outside world know about the kinds of things I had begun studying over the past six years, there was no better way to do it than as a geiko. Instead of hiding myself away in some library somewhere doing academic research, I could communicate with so many more people by continuing my work in the *hanamachi*.

Although they had no immediate affect on my decision to leave, her words must have sunk deep into my consciousness. Only two months before I was supposed to leave the hanamachi, and shortly after I'd begun to make my rounds of the tea houses to express my thanks for their years of support, it suddenly dawned on me how much I loved this world with all its culture and tradition. I thought about all the things I still had to learn and felt ashamed that I'd ever thought I would achieve everything I wanted to achieve in just six years. I decided to tell Koito-san that I wanted to become a geiko—that I would start over from scratch and stay with the okiya for at least another year with the same commitment I had as a beginner. Koito-san accepted my last-minute change of mind and smoothed things over in the hanamachi.

Now I believe that it was my destiny to stay. During the time I was planning on leaving, nothing seemed to be going right, but the moment I made my decision, I felt as if a huge weight had been lifted from my shoulders.

We had to quickly set dates for two special occasions: *sakko*, which is

This was taken on the banks of the Kamo river when I wore the sakko hairstyle. The kimono I'm wearing is a little more grown-up. A maiko is supposed to look cute and childish, whereas a *geiko* should look elegant and grown-up, and the sakko is the period during which we make that change. The formal kimono we wear at this time is very heavy, over thirty pounds. We also wear a special *kanzashi*, which is usually in the shape of a crane or a turtle. My *oneesan* had a special kanzashi made for me in the shape of a treasure ship by a craftsman in Tokyo—it was so beautiful and I felt really proud to wear something so unique. My sakko was at the end of November, just when the leaves were changing color; the falling leaves kind of matched my mood—an end to the old life and a period of preparation for the new.

the final two weeks of a maiko's career, and *erikae*, which is the ceremony that would make me a full geiko. Six years is longer than usual to work as a maiko, and all my maiko "classmates" had already become geiko, so I wanted to have the ceremony as soon as possible. In the end, we decided I would become a full geiko on December 8, 2005, just two months before I had been due to quit.

But first was the period of sakko, which in our geiko house lasts for fifteen days. I would wear a black formal kimono for five days, then a colored one for five days, and then the black one again. Geiko have never been allowed to marry, and in the olden days the sakko served as a kind of alternative wedding ceremony to show they were no longer a child and had become an adult. They wore a bride's traditional hairstyle and adult clothes. Back then, the maiko would have been accompanied by her *danna*, or patron.

Nowadays the sakko period lets everyone know that our life as a maiko will soon be coming to an end. Maiko are supposed to use this time to think hard about the life ahead of them. It was quite an emotional time, looking back over the last five and a half years—knowing that it would soon be over.

When we wear the black kimono, we also follow an old tradition of coloring our teeth black. A long time ago, married women used to blacken their teeth and shave their eyebrows. But blackening my teeth was a total nightmare! The wax has to be applied quickly before it hardens, but it won't stick to the teeth unless they are completely dry. I dried my teeth with tissues before melting the wax with a lighter, picked up a ball of melted wax, removed the tissue from my teeth, and then rubbed the wax all over. I had to do this over and over again. My hands got covered in really hot wax, and I had to use a special brush to get to the small parts of my teeth that I couldn't reach with my fingers. Of course, as soon as I ate anything or drank anything hot, the wax would melt right off, so I couldn't even enjoy the delicious food at the sakko dinner held in my honor. A lot of maiko don't bother coloring their teeth anymore, and some just do it for the last three days or the final day, and I can't say I blame them—I bet the maiko who kept their teeth blackened all through the sakko period ended up losing a lot of weight.

On the final day of the sakko, everybody gathered at the okiya. Then, starting with my *oneesan*, they took turns cutting the topknot of my hair, symbolizing my transition to adulthood. When a maiko becomes a geiko, she wears a wig instead of tying up her own hair, so most choose to cut their hair short before they become a geiko. I loved my long hair, but after six years it was so convenient to have it short. At last I'd be able to wash my hair every day again, instead of just the weekly shampoo I was allowed when I had my hair tied up in the maiko style.

The next day, I went to the salon and had my hair cut properly. It was time for my debut as a geiko.

During my sakko, a new shikomi came to live with us at the *okiya*. It seemed to me like another symbol of the new replacing the old as the old moves on to a new life. Here, I'm just heading out to my first ozashiki of the night. The shikomi help us in lots of small ways, by bringing our bags to the door and things like that.

The collar of our kimono changes to a red and gold combination during sakko, also to make us look more grown-up. The red ball at the back of my hair (LEFT) is called an *akadama*. We often wear these decorations, but during sakko we have a special one made of coral. At the front a red ribbon holds the whole hairstyle together.

All the customers want to see us during our sakko, so it ends up being a really busy time—sometimes I took part in as many as five or six ozashiki in a single day, and I never knew where I was supposed to go next. Sakko is a very special time—there was a strange kind of excitement at all the parties I went to during those two weeks.

The Birth of a Geiko

After performing the traditional sake-drinking ceremony for my *erikae*, I was given a meal full of dishes that symbolize good luck and happiness (RIGHT). Of course, I didn't just sit there and eat it all myself! I shared it with everyone in the *okiya*, and gave the fish, which is the most expensive dish, to my parents.

This fish (LEFT) is called *tai*, and it's something we Japanese eat on special occasions for good luck, first because it tastes really good, and second because its name is similar to the Japanese word *medetai*, which means something like "congratulations."

*O*nce the two weeks of *sakko* were over, it was time for my *erikae*. The erikae is a *geiko*'s debut, just like the *misedashi* is for a *maiko*. Erikae literally means "collar turning," and the moment the maiko exchanges her red collar for the geiko's white one, she becomes an adult member of the *hanamachi*.

I took the day before the ceremony off and spent it in pretty much the same way as I had the day before my misedashi, going around to all the tea houses in the area to let them know about my erikae, having dinner with my parents, and getting everything ready for the big day.

At my misedashi I'd been so nervous I could hardly remember anything about it. Since then I'd seen and taken part in so many ceremonies that they had become a pretty normal part of life for me, and so this time I was able to just relax and enjoy it. I even had a little time to think about all the changes that had occurred in me between the two ceremonies. At my misedashi, I'd had no idea where my life would take me. But by the time of my erikae, I had experienced so much and thought so hard about my decision to become a geiko that I had no reason to feel worried. I knew all the people around me, and everything went exactly according to plan.

Although I was the first maiko to join Koito-san's *okiya*, I was the third to become a fully fledged geiko. My period of service as a maiko had lasted longer than usual, and some maiko who had trained in our okiya ended up becoming geiko before me. In a sense, you could say I was like the oldest daughter who had now become the youngest.

Maybe I should explain this in a little more detail. Whether we are maiko or geiko, what's on the inside is basically the same, but in the hanamachi, the outside is important too. If customers think that one girl looks like a "classic" maiko, she stays a maiko for a longer time. Girls who are thought to look more like geiko will be presented as geiko more quickly. I am short and have a round baby-face, so even though people often tell me I'm quite mature and talk like an adult, I was kept as a maiko. First impressions matter a lot in our world.

The day of my erikae was incredibly busy. As well as attending my evening ozashiki, I had to go around all the tea houses and greet the owners. Thankfully, one of my customers hired a rickshaw for me as a present to save my tired legs! He even had the rickshaw driver wear a coat with the Japanese character for "congratulations." As the driver ran through the streets, the wind blew gently, and since I was sitting up high, I was able to see Miyagawa-cho from a new perspective. It was a great feeling.

Lots of people often commented on how well the members of our okiya got along. My best friend was Kosen-san. We had worked so hard together, and we were both desperate to succeed in the future. Through the years we became pretty close, and we were always holding hands and that kind of thing. Although she had joined the okiya after me, Kosen-chan had her erikae six months earlier, and so she really understood how I felt on the day of the ceremony. Just having her there supporting me really meant a lot.

After the ceremony, once again I had to go around to all the tea houses to greet the owners. This time, though, the tiring job was made a lot more comfortable by the kindness of one of my customers, who—as a present for my erikae—had arranged for me to ride in a rickshaw to spare my having to walk.

I also had many *ozashiki* to attend, but this time I really enjoyed them. By now, I knew most of the customers quite well, and even the people that

The day before my erikae ceremony I had my long hair cut short. (I guess it was probably about six inches longer than this when I was still a *maiko*.) *Geiko* usually wear wigs, which makes things much easier. Having my hair cut made me relieved that I no longer had to look after complicated hairstyles anymore, and at the same time happy that I was entering an adult world.

These are the tools of the *oshiroiya*, the makeup artist. The oshiroiya uses lots of different brushes—some for the face, the smaller ones for details like the eyebrows, some to suit differently shaped faces. The makeup itself is the same as that used by kabuki actors; regular cosmetics stores don't sell it, of course, so we have to go to specialist stores to get our supplies.

I didn't know were well acquainted with the customs. It was completely different from my experience after my misedashi, when I was meeting tons of customers I knew nothing about.

Becoming a geiko was a big relief. We held the erikae in early December, after most of the classes and meetings were done for the year. Of course there were lots of end-of-year parties to keep me busy, but still I felt like I had some time to relax and just enjoy being a geiko. I had also been lucky enough to learn from the experiences of Kosen-san and Yachiho-san—I already knew what kinds of things can be trouble for a new geiko and what was expected of me. I was no longer in uncharted territory.

I also soon realized that ozashiki are completely different for geiko and maiko. Maiko are often just seen as stereotypes; nobody bothers to look beyond the make-up to the real person beneath. A geiko, on the other hand, is seen as an individual with a name and a unique personality. For a maiko, the most important thing is to match the image that people have of us, but as a geiko, it's okay for us to let our own character show. After all my worry about becoming a geiko, I finally felt liberated.

Oshiroi is actually really bad for the skin, so we never use it without brushing a special type of oil onto our face and neck. Then, we put on a two-layer hairnet (LEFT). It's very important to smooth down the hair so that no bumps are left. If you don't do that, the wig doesn't sit properly and it can get really uncomfortable.

After applying the oil and putting on the hairnet, the oshiroi is applied (RIGHT). At first it looks thin and uneven, but the oshiroiya uses her brushes to spread it evenly all over the face and neck.

Erikae is a very important event in the life of a geiko, so on this day the back of the neck is painted in the *sanbonashi* style (FAR RIGHT). For a geiko, the way she looks from behind is just as important as the way she looks from the front.

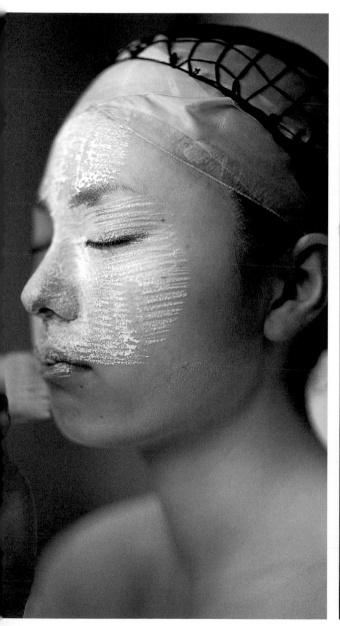

I'm a big fan of my makeup artist—I always watch her closely and try to copy her techniques, but I never do it as well as she does. As a geiko, my makeup changed quite a lot. I started painting my eyebrows shorter than before and using red eyeliner (LEFT) on the corners of my eyes.

Our wigs (ABOVE) are made of human hair and are handmade by specialist craftsmen. They're incredibly expensive, so when they start to get a bit worn, we take them back to the craftsman to get repaired. If we really look after them and get them fixed every five years or so, they can last pretty much a whole lifetime. I have two wigs, both of which were presents from my customers. They are handmade, so they're slightly different, but that means I can switch between them depending on my mood.

My *otokoshi*, here dressing me in my geiko kimono for the first time, looks kind of scary, but he's really a nice guy. My first impression of the geiko-style kimono was how light and comfortable it felt. When I wore my maiko kimono, I was always worried about going downstairs: I had to hold on to my obi to make sure it didn't shift out of place. With the geiko kimono, I no longer had to do that, which was a big relief. This style of kimono isn't completely problem-free, either: at first, my obi always used to ride up whenever I got into and out of cars, another new thing I had to get used to.

This poster (ABOVE) is known as *ohigara*, and it was sent to me to celebrate my erikae. In the olden days, they used to draw a picture of the maiko's face. I've seen some of those old ohigara, and they're really cute. Now, though, they just write the name of the maiko who's becoming a geiko and draw good luck symbols like cranes and turtles.

There are two dishes that are always cooked for erikae: a whole tai and red rice. Here the red rice has been molded with the white rice in the shape of the yin-yang symbol (RIGHT), but every chef has his own technique. The chopsticks are held in a special paper holder tied with a decorative ribbon called a *noshi*. Maybe regular Japanese people don't have so many chances to eat such traditional Japanese food, but maiko and geiko are lucky enough to get to eat this sort of thing on many occasions.

Before the meal, I exchanged sake cups with my
oneesan, like I did at my *misedashi*, and then (ABOVE)
said to her, while bowing, *"Otanamo shimasu."*
Only then were we allowed to eat.

I was only able to nibble a bit—and soon it
was time to go around to the tea houses to greet the
owners. When I stepped outside of the okiya (RIGHT),
there were lots of people waiting for me, cheering
and taking photos.

As I walked around Miyagawa-cho (ABOVE) with my
obachan, all the people who had been waiting
outside the okiya took lots of photos.

As you can see from my face (RIGHT), I'm having
a really good time—so different from my misedashi,
when I was so nervous I couldn't even think straight!
In my right hand I'm holding a special fan called a
kurobone, or "black bone," because the spines are
black instead of the usual white. Every time I greeted
an owner, I had to place it in front of my face and
bow. It's a kind of fixed pattern for greeting people
during erikae, and the kurobone fan is only used at
this time.

A Journey Begins

We pay our respects to the tea houses and teachers whom we're indebted to on August 1, known as *Hassaku*. Some *geiko* and *maiko* from other houses are visiting our *okiya* (LEFT), greeting Koito-san.

This (RIGHT) is a scene from an ozashiki, at which I'm performing with Kosen-san (who is out of the frame) an *itcho-ikkan*, which is a duet for Japanese flute and drum. Of course it's impossible to take along drums and flutes to every ozashiki just in case, so we only perform itcho-ikkan when a customer requests it in advance.

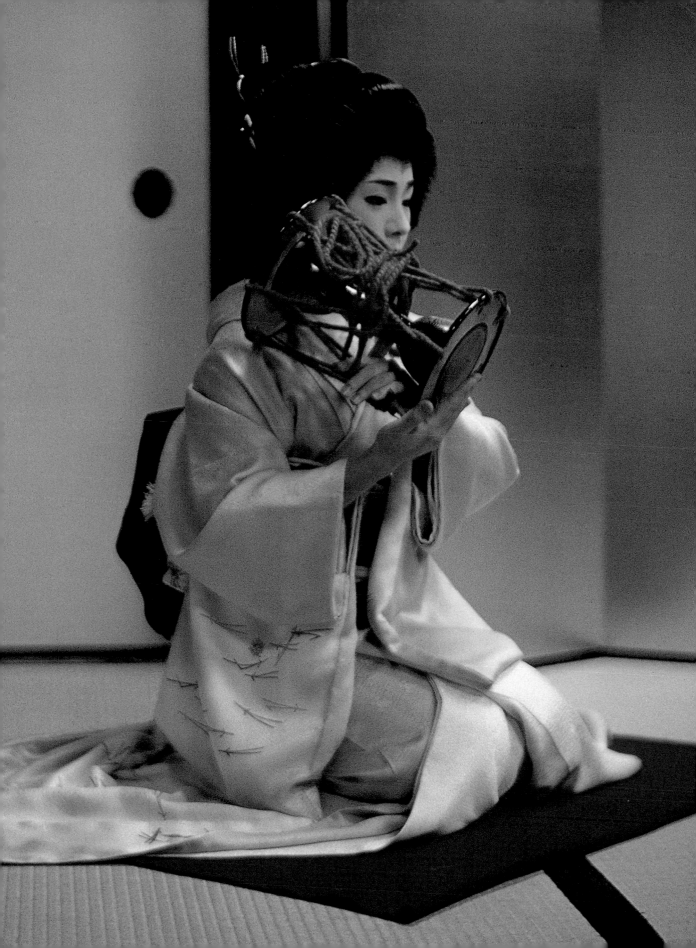

*T*rue to my word, I stayed with the *okiya* for another year, starting my training right back from the start, as if I was a *shikomi* again. My main worry at that time was whether or not I should make the transition to being a fully independent *geiko*—a *jimae*—living away from Koito-san's okiya. I had been there for seven years, so it wasn't an easy decision. I asked for advice from lots of older geiko who had already become independent, and eventually I decided I would give it a try.

Making the decision was one thing, but actually becoming independent was something else entirely. First of all, I needed somewhere to live. My *oneesan* suggested that I should just buy my own house, since monthly mortgage payments would be about the same price as the rent on an apartment. I was really keen on the idea, but finding the right place was hard. I spent two or three months house-hunting every day, but all to no avail. At one point I gave up hope of finding a good house and started searching for an apartment instead, but even that wasn't easy: it was the middle of the moving season and all the good apartments were taken. Eventually, though, I found a nice house and decided that February 20, 2007 would be my last day at the okiya.

There is no particular event or ceremony to mark a geiko's independence—the most stressful thing for me was saying goodbye to Koito-san. For once, though, there was no need to use any formal expressions, so I was able to tell her, from my heart, just how I felt. Our conversation was far more moving than any ceremony I'd ever been through. I thanked her, and asked her to continue to help me in the future. I told her how glad I was that I hadn't quit. She said that because the bath in my new house was small, I was always welcome to use the bath in the okiya. After being in the okiya for my entire career in the *hanamachi*, it was an incredibly lonely feeling—knowing that tomorrow I would be sleeping somewhere else.

Even after I became independent, I still kept my appointment book at the okiya, so I dropped by almost every day. My name, Komomo, was still hung on the door, and if someone wanted to book me for an *ozashiki*, they

I'm now living alone in my own house, but the *otokoshi* still comes and dresses me for special occasions.

had to call the okiya, so in reality, my day-to-day life didn't really change that much. The main difference was in my income. While I was in the okiya, I'd never had to pay for my kimono, but now I would have to pay for them out of my own salary. I also had to start paying for all of my dance lessons. More importantly, I had to take responsibility for my own practice, deciding when to go and creating my own study plan.

Previously, I had handed over my entire earnings to the okiya, and in return, they took care of my food, board, and clothing. Becoming an independent geiko basically meant I became president of my own little business. It was nice to be able to keep all of my earnings from the ozashiki, but harder to figure out how to carefully use this to support, feed, and clothe myself.

Being a geiko has been a truly happy experience for me. I know I would always want to continue my studies in traditional Japanese arts even if I left the world of the hanamachi, but I can't imagine how hard it would be to work a regular nine-to-five job and study at the same time. Even studying one dance would be hard; studying enough to learn three or four would cost all my time and money. In that respect, I can count myself very lucky to be

Just like everything else in our world, there are rules for the way we pour beer. The right hand should be at the top, covering the label, and the left hand below. I'm actually doing it wrong here—my right hand is much too low—but considering that we pour to customers on our left, customers on our right, customers in front of us, and so on and so on, it's almost impossible to get it right every time.

When I became a jimae—a fully independent geiko—a small party was held for me by some of my costumers, and some of my sempai and my oneesan attended. In the picture at left, we're all holding bottles of beer and we're just getting ready to pour them for the customers.

a geiko, making a life for myself by doing something most people can only manage as an expensive hobby.

The ozashiki are exciting, too. The customers' faces when they see the *maiko* and geiko for the first time always make me smile—regardless of whether they're Japanese or foreign, their reaction is always exactly the same! When I talk to foreign customers, even through an interpreter, they often wonder what kind of questions I get asked by the Japanese customers, and I always reply, "Exactly the same kinds of questions you're asking."

Our customers ask all kinds of questions, but because the origins of the geiko world lie in the entertainment of clients by women, this topic comes up particularly often. In Miyagawa-cho there was once a red-light district which existed alongside the geiko district. The geiko and the *shogi*—the prostitutes—worked in the same district, but their jobs were completely separate. The geiko would entertain the customers with their skills in the arts at ozashiki, while the prostitutes entertained their customers in a "different" way later. The geiko were never required to do the job of the shogi.

In 1958 the law was changed to make red-light districts illegal, leaving only the geiko hanamachi in Kyoto. But there are still misunderstandings, and it makes me wish people understood us better. Even Japanese people sometimes think that all geiko still have a *danna*, a rich man who acts as a geiko's patron. It's true that geiko used to depend on a patron, but in the past even ballet dancers, for example, depended on a patron for support.

No matter how skillful, ballet dancers still need some kind of support to pursue their art, and so do we. We don't necessarily need individual patrons, but we do need the support of our customers—and that support can come in various ways, such as giving us a wig or an elegant kimono. (As I mentioned before, you wouldn't believe how much we spend on kimono.)

Now, as a fully fledged member of the hanamachi, I worry about its future. The geiko world has always been a kind of closed-off, hidden place, so few people know very much about it. They don't know the difference between a maiko and a geiko; some don't even know anything about kimono and Japanese arts. Just to use the example of kimono again: One of my worries is that since so few people wear kimono anymore, the number of kimono makers is decreasing; and because our kimono are specially made, they are becoming more and more expensive. If the number of ozashiki and other events decrease we will never be able to afford them, so it's very important to keep the hanamachi as a vibrant part of Japanese culture.

Yet it's no exaggeration to say that the hanamachi are suffering, and if nothing is done, they could cease to exist. They will become just like an art exhibition or a museum exhibit. I can't bear to think that we might lose this world. My biggest dream is for the hanamachi to become a normal part of ordinary people's lives, and I am always thinking about what I can do to make that dream come true.

This is one of the little shrines dedicated to the Jizo bodhisattva, at the time of the Jizo Bon festival in the latter half of August. Jizo is best known as a guardian of children.

After one year as a geiko, I was able to get my own house and had the interior redecorated. I felt a bit lonely at first, but at the same time I was really proud of my little house.

The Takase Canal (LEFT) is only a few minutes walk from Miyagawa-cho. When these cherry trees blossom in spring, it's a beautiful sight.

The Kaburenjo in Miyagawa-cho (ABOVE) is such a beautiful old building—I feel incredibly lucky to be able to study dance here. Whenever I walk past it I get a really strong sense of the history and culture of the hanamachi.

PAGES 130–131 (COUNTERCLOCKWISE, FROM TOP LEFT): Each of us has a *getabako*, or shoebox, in the Kaburenjo. The floor of the practice space is concrete, and if we wear *okobo* on it, they get damaged, so we put our outdoor shoes in the box and change into *zori*, which are sandals made of straw. Geiko don't have to wear okobo anymore, so it's really only maiko who use the getabako every day.

At the beginning and end of every practice, we have to bow to the master.

The style of the bow is so important—we have to take great care that our bottom doesn't rise up. There's an old word for bottom—*oido*—and from our very first day as a *shikomi*, we're always being told not to lift up our oido! We spend a lot of time bowing, not just during practice but also at the beginning and end of every performance.

We usually learn new dances in two stages. In the first stage, the master stands next to us and shows us how to stand and how to move. We copy her movements and try to remember them. In the second stage, the master sits down and we perform what we've learned. She lets us know what we're not getting right until we've perfected the dance. The dance I'm learning here is a summer dance called Uchimizu, based on the Japanese custom of sprinkling water onto streets and gardens to ease the heat.

On the night of *setsubun*, a ceremony to chase away devils and welcome good spirits, we dress up in crazy costumes. The night is called *obake* (ghost), and it's always a lot of fun. I'm dressed up as Otomisan (BELOW), a character from an old Tokyo kabuki play about two lovers who are separated from each other. As you can see, she has no eyebrows, which was the custom for married women in the old days.

The three of us went to lots of ozashiki in our costumes (TOP RIGHT) on that night. We always have to make ourselves beautiful in our everyday life, so obake is the only time we're allowed to purposely

look a mess, so you can imagine that there's a lot of competition for the male roles!

On this night, we ended up showing our faces at more than seventy ozashiki. Of course, we have something to drink at each one, so we end up a little tipsy, to say the least. We carried props for our skits (BOTTOM RIGHT), but ended up forgetting them at several of the ozashiki as we got drunker and drunker! By the end of the night we were pretty much adlibbing the whole thing, but the customers didn't seem to mind. Maybe because they were drunker than us!

Here I'm putting on makeup as a geiko, just before putting on my wig, and even I can see the difference in my facial expression compared to when I was a maiko. I'm using the same mirror I used as a maiko, which I got from my oneesan after she said she didn't want it anymore. I've tried other, newer mirrors, but this one, even though it's a bit worn, is still the easiest for me to use.

PAGES 136–137: The streets of Miyagawa-cho used to be made of asphalt, but a few years ago the city of Kyoto helped the neighborhood redo them in stone, which goes so much better with the look of the street—and the *chochin* lanterns of the tea houses. I think people are surprised to find the unhurried atmosphere of the hanamachi only a short distance from Kyoto's center.

I'm wearing a simple *karage*-style kimono here, so I guess I must be taking a breather before getting ready to go out to my evening ozashiki. I look deep in thought; I wonder what on earth I was thinking about. . . .

AFTERWORD

I first crossed paths with the young Japanese girl who was to become the *geiko* Komomo at the Kaden geiko house in Miyagawa-cho, Kyoto. Her name was Ruriko and she was visiting from China, where her family was living at the time. She was making use of a brief return to Japan to visit and get a feel for life in the *hanamachi*. It was the spring of 1999, and in the small reception room of the *okiya*, she looked as incongruous as Alice on her first day in Wonderland. Yet, even now, I can remember being struck by the glow of determination in her eyes.

I was still at university, studying physics, but I was on my own mission. For a long time I had been entranced by the beauty of kimono, not to mention the elegant movement of the women wearing them, and it had always been a dream of mine to capture this beauty with my camera. My search for that, sadly, now rare species—women who wear kimono every day—is what led me to the hanamachi of Kyoto and the *maiko-san* living and working in the district.

I asked the *okami*-san, the owner of the okiya, for permission to speak to the young girl. We found that we had much in common—both of us had lived overseas and, as a result of our experiences, had both been drawn to the traditional culture of our native land. It was not long into the conversation before I was convinced that she would achieve her dream of becoming a maiko. I suddenly asked her if she would mind me visiting her in China, thinking how interesting it would be to capture photos of the daily life of a Japanese girl living in another country and dreaming of becoming a maiko.

Nine years on, this collection of photographs has come together in book form. I asked Momo-chan, as she is now known to her friends, to let me subject her to a series of interviews in order to provide some context about her thoughts and feelings at the times the photographs were taken. During the interviews, which ultimately stretched on for many hours, I realized that these were the first real conversations we'd had since I visited her in China.

More than a hundred times over as many months I had made the round trip from my home in Nagoya to Kyoto, and followed quietly by her side as she worked her way through the stresses and strains of life in the strange netherworld of Miyagawa-cho. My aim was to capture her in those moments when the essence of her beauty was brought to life as she grew up by the mysterious culture of the hanamachi, and both that beauty and the mystery is what I hope to convey in this book.

As a result, our conversations were almost completely limited to "Hello" and "How are you?" Instead, I allowed my eyes to do the talking, always searching for hints of beauty so elusive that Momo-chan herself was often unaware of their presence. When I finally exchanged my camera for a tape recorder and began the interviews, I was both surprised and delighted as I rediscovered this young woman in the world of words.

Only the privileged and connected few ever have the chance to attend an *ozashiki*, and beyond those tea house parties, the geiko and maiko live in an even more secretive world, completely closed to outsiders. Their day-to-day life is far off-limits even to their customers, let alone the average person.

So why was I allowed to enter this world when only very few of my fellow Japanese photographers have been able to gain access? The answer to this question lies not with me, but with the people of Miyagawa-cho, who were kind enough to let me in. As long as they permit me, I will continue to take their photographs.

Naoyuki Ogino, September 2007

ACKNOWLEDGMENTS

First and foremost, I would like to thank Koito-san, who, like a mother, guided me through the world of the *hanamachi*, and in the process taught me a great deal about life. She was also kind enough to write the foreword to this book.

I also owe a huge debt of gratitude to the geiko Komomo-san, who over the years has brought much happiness into my life. If the photographs in this book receive any recognition, it is all because of her. From the early days in China to the present, not once has she refused my requests for new photographs, and she was also kind enough to sit for the long interviews that form the basis of the text in this book.

The *geiko* and *maiko* of Kosen-san, Yachiho-san, and Yasuha-san were also kind enough to allow me to photograph them again and again over the years. And Tsubokura-san, the president of the Miyagawa-cho Union, gave his understanding to this project.

Thanks go also to dance master Yumiji Wakayanagi, who kindly gave her permission for me to photograph dance practice, and all the kind people of Miyagawa-cho who let me take hundreds of photos in and around the hanamachi.

I am also extremely grateful to Mr. and Mrs. Nasu, Momo-chan's father and mother, for their unfailing support from my first, rather sudden, appearance on their doorstep in Beijing to the present day. Thanks also to Mitsuru Ohmura, who kindly put me up in his home in Osaka many times during my numerous trips to Kyoto, and to my fellow photographer Masaaki Morita for his invaluable comments on my work.

To my wife Miki, who uncomplainingly allowed me to pursue my work and understands me better than anyone in the world, and to my parents Michihiro and Hiroko and my sister Marina—who have always shown their support—I am eternally grateful.

I also thank Gregory Starr, my editor at Kodansha International, who understands the power of photography and has guided me carefully, with much positive encouragement even in the face of my stubbornness, through the long period of preparation for publication.

Many others have lent their support to this book in many ways, including Miwako Sato, who introduced my photographs of Komomo in *Kateigaho International* magazine. I am grateful to them all.

（英文版）芸妓小桃　A Geisha's Journey

2008年1月25日　第1刷発行

写　真　　荻野NAO之
テキスト　小桃
発行者　　富田 充
発行所　　講談社インターナショナル株式会社

〒112-8652 東京都文京区音羽1-17-14
電話　03-3944-6493（編集部）
　　　03-3944-6492（営業部・業務部）
ホームページ　www.kodansha-intl.com

印刷・製本所　大日本印刷株式会社